Original title:
Butterflies and Roses

Copyright © 2024 Creative Arts Management OÜ
All rights reserved.

Author: Daisy Parker
ISBN HARDBACK: 978-9916-94-774-6
ISBN PAPERBACK: 978-9916-94-775-3

The Flight of Tenderness

In gardens where the giggles bloom,
A dance unfolds, dispelling gloom.
With fluttering wings and airy toes,
They prance around in silly rows.

A petal's hat, they wear askew,
Each twist and turn, a comical view.
They hop like clowns on springs so bright,
Creating laughs in pure delight.

With colors bold, they tease the sun,
A chase ensues, it's all in fun.
A bloom gives chase, a playful game,
In this odd drama, none feel shame.

So join the quirky, floral chase,
Where whimsy finds the silliest place.
In every flap, a hearty cheer,
For joy and laughter are always near.

Fluttering Elegance

In the garden, a dance so spry,
They twirl and spin as the bees buzz by.
With polka-dot wings and giggles loud,
They'd make the sunbeam blush and proud.

A leap, a bound, over the greens,
In their tiny world, they're the queens.
They sip from cup-shaped blooms aflame,
While teasing rude ants; oh, what a game!

Garden of Grace

Petals wear smiles, colors so bright,
Wobbling creatures take off in flight.
With a hop and a skip, they play chase,
Laughter spills out from their floral space.

They slide on dew drops, such a fun ride,
As the sun's warm glare becomes their guide.
Amidst laughter, whispers, and cute little fights,
The garden's their stage, oh what delights!

Crimson Kisses

They flutter and flap, with mischief in tow,
Like surprise party guests, putting on a show.
In a whirlwind of colors, quite the sight,
They land on the blooms, feeling just right.

With each little whisper, a tickle and tease,
They giggle through petals, dancing with ease.
Oh, what a frolic, such a delight,
As they celebrate life, from morning to night!

Flight of the Enchanted

Through gardens of laughter, the merry prance,
They flit and they flutter, what a chance!
With cheeks rosy red and stripes so bold,
They weave through the air, a sight to behold.

With every wild twirl, they gather some glee,
Transforming a dull day into pure jubilee.
And as the sun sets on their silly spree,
They wink at the stars, 'Come join us, maybe?'

Swaying in the Sunlight

In the garden, things get silly,
The bees dance, looking quite frilly.
Among the blooms, they toss and sway,
As if they're out to steal the day.

A creature flutters, what a sight,
Wings like confetti in pure delight.
Tickling petals, they make a fuss,
As if nature's one big circus bus.

Nature's Gentle Embrace

In a lush patch, colors play,
The scent of mischief floats their way.
A gentle poke from a thorny friend,
Tells all that laughter is on the mend.

Chasing shadows, they spin and glide,
While a ladybug takes a ride.
Giggles echo from everyone around,
In nature's heart, joy is found.

Velvet Transitions

A rustle here, a giggle there,
In shades of velvet, lights declare.
Muffled whispers in the green,
A secret world of mischief seen.

With each sway, the moments tease,
Petals fall, and then there's bees.
They zoom past in a hasty race,
Was that a flower or a hiding face?

Echoes of Enchantment

They flit about, a playful crew,
In patterns that seem so askew.
Chasing laughter through the air,
While flowers giggle without a care.

Caught in a twirl, the colors clash,
Pink and yellow go for a splash.
Underneath this vibrant show,
Who knew blossoms could steal the show?

Petal Dust and Charm

In a garden where giggles bloom,
A flower sneezed, oh what a zoom!
With pollen flying everywhere,
They danced around without a care.

A ladybug lost its cool,
It slipped on dew, oh what a fool!
The daisies giggled, deep in thought,
While the pansies plotted a silly plot.

The Arc of a Gentle Breeze

There once was a wind with a cheeky grin,
It tickled the petals like it was a whim.
They swayed and spun in a playful trance,
While the bees joined in for a wild dance.

A rose tried a waltz, but stepped on a bee,
It buzzed in surprise, "You stepped on me!"
The lilies laughed, in delight they spun,
Chasing each other, all just for fun.

The Language of Blush

A tulip blushed as the sun shone bright,
It whispered to daisies, "Is this too much light?"
The violets chuckled, "Oh, darling, no!"
While sunflowers posed, putting on a show.

Petals spoke softly with colors so grand,
In a tongue only flowers could understand.
But a breeze interrupted, with a silly jest,
Leaving everyone giggling, they seemed so blessed.

Adventure in Papillon

A little creature with colors so bright,
Wore polka dots and danced with delight.
It flitted about, causing a fuss,
"I'm the star here! Make way for us!"

But tripped on a petal, oh what a scene,
Did a somersault, it was quite the routine!
The roses all laughed at its clumsy affair,
And joined in the fun with a flurry of flair.

Radiance Among Thorns

In gardens where the giggles grow,
An insect dance, a vibrant show.
With secret winks and tiny prances,
They flutter 'round like silly lances.

The petals blush, a cheeky sight,
In shades so bold, they're quite a fright.
That's nature's jest, oh what a tease,
With thorns that poke, yet bring such ease.

The Language of Petals and Wings

A buzz of gossip in the air,
As blossoms wink, with petals bare.
They whisper tales of pollen trails,
And cheeky smirks amid the gales.

Two wings collide, a clumsy dance,
They swirl and swirl, without a chance.
A blooper reel in sunny skies,
Where nature laughs and giggles rise.

A Tapestry of Flora

In patterns bright, the colors weave,
With every twist, it's hard to believe.
A canvas stitched with zest and flair,
Where floral jokes hang in the air.

An awkward bloom that trips a time,
While others roll in colors prime.
The laughter grows, the sun will tease,
In this wild world of floral wheeze.

Cherished Colors

Oh hues that turn a blush to grin,
With silly tricks that draw you in.
Each shade a laugh, a playful song,
In this bright world, we all belong.

But watch your step, the laughter flows,
Among the pranksters, laugh it goes.
With petals soft and laughter loud,
Let's dance around, be silly and proud.

Fluttering Kaleidoscope

A flurry of colors brings laughter,
Dancing on air, a whimsical rafter.
Stomachs are tickled, the breeze is divine,
As petals pirouette with a silly design.

Catching the sunlight, they dart with a grin,
Whispering secrets, where do they begin?
A chuckle erupts as they playfully sway,
In a garden of giggles, they'll frolic and play.

With antics so silly, they tease and they tease,
Hovering close to the tourists' knees.
In a twinkle of laughter, they zoom and they freeze,
A kaleidoscope's charm that aims to please.

Each landing a question, each flutter a jest,
The blooms shake their heads in a floral fest.
A whimsical sight, a comedy show,
In this garden, the humor will grow!

Inflorescence

In a parade of colors, what a delight,
Flirting with sunshine, oh what a sight!
A carnival blooms with a giggling flair,
Where petals pop jokes, and pollen fills air.

"Hey! Catch me if you can!" they tease with a dance,
As bees roll their eyes, lost in a trance.
Bumbling and stumbling, they all play along,
In this flowery jest, nothing feels wrong.

With whispers of mischief wrapped up in the breeze,
Cleaning off dew with the greatest of ease.
A party of colors, sprouting with glee,
When life's just a joke, there's no need to flee.

They chuckle in rhythm, as shadows play tricks,
In the garden of laughter, the humor still kicks.
A spectacular banquet of fun on display,
Where blossoms and joy dance the day away!

A Memory in Bloom

Once a shy bud with secrets to share,
Now busting with stories and vibrant flair.
"Do you remember when it was just me?
Now look at us all, we're the life of the spree!"

Like giggling youngsters in springtime's embrace,
With softness and charm, we all find our place.
Trading old tales in a colorful spin,
As time drifts away with each chuckle and grin.

We laugh at the raindrops, the bees, and the sun,
In this jovial bunch, we're just here for fun.
Each petal a giggle, a memory spun,
In a silly old garden, where joy never shuns.

Oh, how the blossoms paraded their jest,
Funky and daring, they're humor at best.
With laughter surrounding, we bloom and we play,
In this cheerful bouquet, let's frolic away!

Enveloping Luminescence

In the twilight of giggles, a glow starts to creep,
Where whispers of humor stir dreams from their sleep.
A lamp of soft colors, casting a jest,
In the hearts of the blooms, a delightful fest.

Dancing on petals, like fireflies bright,
Each flicker a pun, a whimsical flight.
Stirring up chuckles with every soft sway,
In an echo of laughter, the night melts away.

Beneath the soft moonlight, they share silly tales,
Of mugging with bumblebees and wobbly trails.
Layers of humor, spun into the night,
Where every new flutter brings joy to the sight.

With joy wrapped in colors, a hilarious tease,
They lift up their spirits, and dance in the breeze.
An enveloping glow, a luminous cheer,
In this whimsical haven, we all gather near!

The Fluttering Secret

In a garden full of giggles,
Tiny critters do their dance,
With grace and flair, they wiggle,
In a whirlwind, they prance.

They wear their stripes and spots,
Like fashion from a dream,
Whispering silly thoughts,
In the sunlight, they gleam.

A secret shared with blooms,
Of laughter in the air,
They flip and flop in rooms,
Of petals everywhere.

They tease with their bright flutters,
Causing roses to blush red,
In this floral, funny mutters,
Laughter fills the garden bed.

Blossoms and Transformations

Once a worm, now a maestro,
Conducting blooms with flair,
He twirls in grand ol' show,
While petals toss their hair.

The laughter fills the breeze,
As flowers start to sway,
Rolling with giggles and ease,
In a vibrant ballet.

With every turn and twist,
The colors burst and beam,
Nature's funny little tryst,
A whimsical daydream.

Through gardens they exclaim,
In a dance, they joke and poke,
About their fancy names,
And the coffee they all smoke.

A Tapestry of Grace

In the tapestry of spring,
Threads of laughter intertwine,
With colors bright, they cling,
To petals, sun, and wine.

They flap their wings in glee,
As they sip on morning dew,
Making jokes just for thee,
As if beauty's just a cue.

With each light-hearted jest,
The flowers start to giggle,
In nature's charming quest,
They join the dance and wiggle.

A tapestry of fun,
Woven with joy and jest,
In the warm and shining sun,
They put laughter to the test.

Chasing Dappled Light

In the sun's soft embrace,
They flit with silly grace,
Chasing rays of playful shine,
In a world that's truly fine.

Oh, the drapes of shadows fall,
As they play the game of tag,
With flowers standing tall,
While giggles fill the rag.

Dappled beams like confetti,
Scatter on leafy greens,
As laughter grows quite heady,
Amidst the floral scenes.

Beyond the blooms, they whirl,
In a dance that takes a flight,
Painting joy with every twirl,
In the chase of dappled light.

The Creative Blossom

In a garden wild, where giggles bloom,
A jester hops, dispelling gloom.
Petals dance in the sun's warm light,
While bees join in with their buzz, what a sight!

A tulip wore a hat, oh so grand,
A daisy twirled, a new dance planned.
Laughter echoed, the sun started to sway,
As blooms told jokes in their own silly way.

The daisies shared tales of a lost shoe,
While the violets painted skies so blue.
A sunflower winks, with seeds it can toss,
As petals create a confetti gloss.

Every bud chuckled 'neath verdant leaves,
Tickling the breeze, sharing their thieves.
In this colorful show, no need to rush,
For every flower knows how to make a fuss.

Kaleidoscope Soul

In acid greens and skies of teal,
A twist of humor, oh what a deal!
Petals giggle with the sun's warm rays,
Whirling and twirling in fabulous ways.

A ladybug's on a wild trip too,
Trading its spots for a polka-dot shoe.
In this kaleidoscope of fragrant delight,
Giggling blooms party, from morning till night.

The poppies prance in polka-dot dance,
While hummingbirds try their best to prance.
Each bloom a jester in colors so bright,
With punchlines spilling in the soft twilight.

As laughter leads through the floral maze,
A world full of fun, in whimsical haze.
So come join the jest, feel the essence roll,
In this garden of joy, with a kaleidoscope soul.

Echoes in the Garden

A squirrel spills the beans with a grin,
As roses whisper secrets to wind that's thin.
Petals giggle at clouds in the sky,
When daisies jump up, and the bluebirds fly.

The garden chimes with laughter and glee,
As a bee waltzes close to a flamboyant pea.
A butterfly knows all the jokes to share,
While sleeping blooms snore without a care.

In corners where shadows of blooms intertwine,
Chortles arise from each vine, how divine!
A chorus of chirps wraps around the grass,
In a concert of giggles, the moments pass.

Each leaf is a witness, each bud has a role,
In the echo of laughter, the garden, a soul.
So tiptoe through petals, and never feel down,
For humor is planted in every town.

Sunlit Reveries

In a daydreaming patch where laughter takes flight,
Sunbeams tickle blooms, what a fun sight!
Lilies play hopscotch on the soft, green lawn,
While daisies cheer for the sun to keep on.

With every bright color, mischief invites,
Gardeners giggle, armed with their tights.
A raucous parade of stems in a beat,
Strutting their stuff on the sun-kissed street.

The marigolds gawk at the butterflies' spin,
Who flit in and out with their cheeky grin.
Petals perching on each other's toes,
In the rhythm of nature, anything goes!

With laughter, they sway in the breeze's embrace,
In this sunlit reverie, find your happy place.
Join the flower party, come sway and hum,
For in this wild garden, we all are just fun!

Velvet Caresses

In a garden where laughter does fly,
Petals tumble, oh my, oh my!
With winks from the blooms, they sway in delight,
While ants do the tango, oh what a sight!

Silly little critters, they dance with such glee,
Daffodils giggle as they sip on their tea.
Mice wear tiny hats, oh what a parade,
In this floral fiesta, no one feels afraid!

Ephemeral Beauty's Embrace

The sneaky breeze tickles the cheek,
As petals whisper secrets, oh so unique.
Bumbles buzzing like they own the place,
While ladybugs strut with a fabulous grace!

Pollen fights back with a tickling charm,
It pulls at the nose, causing quite the alarm.
"God bless you!" we say, with a grin and a laugh,
As flower-dusted giggles float down the path!

Wings of an Afternoon

A tiny riddle flits through the sky,
With colors so bright, it's a rainbow's ally.
Giggles escape from blooms when they tease,
Planting wild jokes on the hummingbird breeze!

In a wacky world of fragrance and flair,
A squirrel juggles nuts without a care.
But shh! The roses plot with the sun,
To paint the whole garden with a whimsical fun!

Blooms of a Thousand Dreams

In the garden of wishes, what do we see?
Flowers in hats, as jolly as can be!
A cactus in shades, trying hard to fit in,
While daisies hold court with a court jester's grin!

The sun starts to set, it's time for a show,
The petals belt out tunes, with a glowing afflow.
What a sight it is, oh such a winning scheme,
In this meadow of laughter and whimsical dreams!

A Cascade of Color

In gardens bright with hues so bold,
Squishy bugs in their flapping gold.
They dance like fools on summer's stage,
With moves that might entice a sage.

Their laughter echoes in the sun,
Who knew that insects could have fun?
They sip sweet nectar, all a-flurry,
While blooms just watch, without a worry.

The Hidden Moth's Song

A shy one lurks in twilight's scene,
Wings like shadows, soft and keen.
She hums a tune of gooey dreams,
While flowers giggle in their creams.

The night is full of jiggles and japes,
As furry friends make funny shapes.
They flit and twirl, a silly gang,
While nature laughs and softly sang.

Transient Love

They flirt and dash from bud to bud,
In this garden realm of pollen and mud.
A flicker here, a flutter there,
Their romance blooms in the warm, sweet air.

But just like that, they're off again,
Chasing sunshine, leaves, and rain.
Oh, fleeting love, do come and stay,
But laughter rules when you fly away!

The Poetry of Transformation

From drab to fab in a blink of eye,
Dancing in skirts, they reach for the sky.
Once little lumps, now vibrant spark,
They tease and twirl till it's completely dark.

Their art is born in the breeze so light,
With every flap, they feel so right.
Oh, what a shift from dull to bold,
With nature's humor in every fold!

Whispers of Color

In gardens where the petals tease,
Little critters play with ease.
With twirls and swirls, a lively dance,
They prance around, not left to chance.

A tickle here, a nudge there,
They flaunt their hues, without a care.
One lands atop a sneaky nose,
Who knew this would provoke some woes?

Petals in the Breeze

A gentle gust, a dizzy spin,
Petals fly like they're in a win.
With cheeky grins, they swirl about,
Who needs a reason? They just shout!

An intruder stops to take a snap,
But the petals plot their little map.
They swirl around and hold their breath,
Oh dear, that's one way to tease death!

Dance of the Delicate Wings

Wings flitter by, oh what a sight,
They gossip loudly, day and night.
A bloom blushes, feeling quite bold,
As whispers of color unfold.

One zips past with a zany flair,
Landing on a wonky hair.
The owner shrieks, "What's stuck to me?"
A giggling crew, how can this be?

Blooming Dreams

In gardens where the laughs bloom bright,
Creatures dance, a silly flight.
With every flap, a jest in tow,
They flutter soft, and steal the show.

A rose blushes, shy from the crowd,
While antics catch the eye, so loud.
"Don't eat me!" cries the leafy friend,
But here they thrive, a comic blend!

Songs of the Meadow

In the field, they dance with flair,
Making even daisies stare.
A jig so silly, bright and bold,
They twirl in colors, pure and gold.

With winks and giggles in the breeze,
They tease the flowers, if you please.
Jumping high, then falling low,
In pollen parties, they steal the show!

Round and round, a merry race,
They land with laughter, full of grace.
A game of tag, they never tire,
While sunbeams cheer and sing in choir.

So raise a toast to this delight,
Where wings collide and hearts take flight.
In meadows green, with nectar sweet,
It's nature's party—join the beat!

Colorful Embrace

In a garden where colors laugh,
A polka-dotted comedy half.
They flutter here and flap around,
Until they tumble to the ground.

With shades of pink and hints of blue,
They play hide-and-seek, enjoy the view.
Whispers of petals, giggles abound,
In vibrant chaos, joy's the sound.

A bloom proposes a cheeky dance,
While neighbors peek, they take a chance.
Each spin and swirl, a blooming jest,
In nature's comedy, they're the best!

So let the colors paint the air,
With jests and jives they bind their pair.
In laughter's bloom, no need for fears,
A funny saga of sunny cheers!

A Winged Serenade

With flutters and giggles on a quest,
A serenade of nonsense, they jest.
Wings like sketches, a doodle in flight,
In serenades under soft moonlight.

They hover near blooms, a comical sway,
Making blossoms giggle, "Hey, come play!"
A chorus of hues, a prancing scene,
Where petals chuckle, oh so keen.

In tangled vines, they start to twirl,
Each twist a laugh, each leap a whirl.
With tiny jokes and winks so sly,
They serenade stars in the night sky.

So join the fun, let laughter bloom,
Where nonsense reigns in fragrant room.
With cheerful wings and hearts that sing,
In the softest night, let joy take wing!

The Softest Caress

On gentle whispers, they glide with ease,
Playing tag with the summer breeze.
Tickling petals, oh what a ruckus,
A giggle fest, no one can fuss!

With every flutter and cheeky prance,
They find themselves in a merry dance.
Belly laughs echo from leaf to leaf,
In this sweet, silly moment, find relief.

They sway with grace by the old oak tree,
While buds roll their eyes, "Oh, let it be!"
A peptalk here and a nudge on the way,
In nature's circus, join the play!

So tip your hat to this cozy affair,
With softest caress, take joy to share.
Let laughter blossom, let the fun unfurl,
In every nook of this whimsical world!

Hidden Encounters

In gardens where giggles take flight,
A sneaky critter, oh what a sight!
Sipping on nectar, tip-toe in glee,
Whispers of petals, a joke in the spree.

With a blink and a flutter, they tease the man,
Who swats at the air like a crazed little fan.
He slips on a dew, does a silly dance,
Oh, how the blossoms just giggle and prance.

Two blooms exchange jokes with the sun overhead,
As bees start to chuckle at things that they said.
In a world full of laughter, secrets unfold,
When nature's comedians boldly are bold.

So watch for the antics where colors collide,
In the mishaps of nature, with joy as a guide.
A place where the rare meets a tickle of fate,
And each hidden moment ignites laughter's state.

Prayer of the Delicate

Oh, tiny wonders, float on the breeze,
Do you hear us giggle, oh, bring us to knees?
In petals adorned, so graceful and bright,
We wish for your humor to fill up our night.

With glittering wings, while our hearts steal a glance,
Please bless every garden with whimsical dance.
We pray for the laughter that pops like a bloom,
A ticklish tick-tock in the silence's room.

In fragrant confession, the flowers will say,
Life's jokes are the treasures we stumble on play.
So whisper your secrets to petals so fair,
And watch as we chuckle beyond every care.

Oh, soft little wonders, we call on your cheer,
Guide us with laughter, let joy disappear.
In delicate blooms, as the evening grows dark,
May the punchlines of nature delight like a spark.

Ascending Petals

A little green sprite, in the air with a spin,
Plays hopscotch on blossoms, with laughter to win.
She tumbles through giggles, a whirl of delight,
As petals inflate and take off in their flight.

Upward they soar, in a rainbow of glee,
A soft sea of colors is all that they see.
The air fills with chuckles, a feast for the soul,
As blooms twist and turn like they're out on a stroll.

Each petal a punchline, so witty and bright,
While insects applaud, what a marvelous sight!
They swing from the stems like they're going to fall,
In a circus of colors, the funniest ball.

So open the skies for the humor and cheer,
Let us savor each moment, each giggle we hear.
With every ascent, may we float to new heights,
Where wrinkles from laughter unfold in the nights.

Dance of the Vibrant Soul

When colors collide, it's a riotous jam,
A jester of flowers, oh there goes my glam!
With each tiny twirl, they shimmy and sway,
As nature's comedians frolic and play.

The sun starts to chuckle, the clouds raise a brow,
"Who knew they were so good? Look at them now!"
With a flutter and flip, there's quite the commotion,
A ballet of mishaps, oh such a devotion!

The grass starts to giggle, the bugs all applaud,
As petals take center stage, oh look at that broad!
A whirl and a twirl, the shadows catch light,
Each colorful dancer steals wishes from night.

So here's to the show, let it roll on and on,
A chuckle with petals, till daylight is gone.
With every adventure, we rise and we sway,
In the dance of the vibrant, forever we'll play.

Embrace of the Color-Filled Sky

In gardens where the giggles play,
Tiny dancers prance away.
With wings like laughter, bright and free,
They tickle flowers, just to tease.

Petals blush with playful grins,
As buzzing friends hum funny sins.
A swirling dance of silly cheer,
Nature's jesters, always near.

The sky bursts forth in hues galore,
While fluffy clouds begin to snore.
With every bounce and silly twist,
Who knew the blooms could dance like this?

So let's embrace this color spree,
With joy as vast as the open sea.
Laughing friends in prismatic flight,
What a scene, oh, what a sight!

Veils of Color

In gardens draped with vibrant lace,
Colors mingle in a race.
Petals gossip, share their jokes,
While lazy bees sip nectar strokes.

A dandelion wearing shades,
In this garden, wacky parades.
Tickled leaves in the gentle breeze,
Dance with giggles among the trees.

Yellow Suns and Pink Moon's tease,
Encourage blooms to say 'Woohoo!'
As petals flutter, they conspire,
To dress the world in laughable fire.

What a sight, that painted cheer,
In every corner, fun draws near!
Veils of laughter drape the ground,
In this crazy floral playground.

The Journey of Light and Fragrance

A tiny traveler sets the scene,
With quirky steps, and wings so keen.
Through fragrant paths, with laughter bright,
They zip and zoom in the warm sunlight.

Each bloom offers a laugh so sweet,
A ticklish petal, dancing feet.
The world ignites with colors bold,
And thinks of stories yet untold.

With every hop and silly dive,
Joy bursts forth, the plants come alive!
They spin around with fragrant sighs,
Creating happiness that flies.

So join the fun, no time to waste,
In this journey, life's sweet taste.
A tale of giggles, light, and cheer,
Where every sniff brings smiles near!

A Colorful Awakening

When morning rays begin to hum,
A waking world full of fun.
The garden shakes off sleepy yawn,
In riotous hues, new day is born.

Pinks and yellows have a chat,
"Who wore it best?" asks cheeky sprat.
With laughter bursting from each bud,
They swirl and twirl in morning mud.

A playful breeze tickles the cheeks,
And leaves join in with little squeaks.
All around, the colors blend,
With giggles shared, no time to spend.

So here's to mornings bright and merry,
In the gardens, joy they carry.
Every petal sings to say,
"Wake up, world, it's time to play!"

Secrets of the Colorful Dance

In gardens where laughter twirls and spins,
Little creatures with buzzes and grins.
They flit and they flutter, a comic parade,
Chasing the sun, in a jovial charade.

With pockets of petals, they scheme and they plot,
A banquet of nectar, oh what a lot!
They tickle the flowers, they kiss and they tease,
As if nature's giggles dance in the breeze.

In shades of the rainbow, they've taken their flight,
Turning dull blooms into a magical sight.
With every soft landing, they tumble and glide,
Creating a circus, a fanciful ride.

So if you find laughter among the bright blooms,
Remember it's nature that lightens our rooms.
For the secrets they share, with each silly sway,
Are the giggles of spring on a bloom-thrifty day.

Fragile Elegance

In the garden of giggles, they sway and they swirl,
Dressed up in colors, oh watch how they twirl!
Delicate dancers with mischief in sight,
Tickling the petals, oh what a delight!

Each flutter a whisper, each loop a sly game,
They flirt with the blooms, but never the same.
With a wink and a nudge, they dance through the petals,
Their antics bring chuckles, like giggling kettles.

They sip from the treasures, but never too long,
Like playful musicians, they hum a light song.
With elegance fragile, they grace every scene,
A comedic ballet, like no one's unseen.

They jest with the wind, in dramatic display,
Unruly little jesters in a colorful fray.
For even the blooms with their heads held up high,
Can't help but chuckle at the show in the sky.

The Blooming Mirage

Appearing like magic, they shimmer and tease,
Colors exploding like fireworks in trees.
A trickster's delight, they dance on a dare,
Two steps forward, then out of thin air!

They flutter and flitter with whimsical grace,
Playing hide and seek in a flowery race.
With every soft landing, they change the hue,
Painting the world with their mischief anew.

In gardens of laughter, where silliness reigned,
They create a mirage where giggles have gained.
A hop and a skip, they sing their sweet song,
Inviting the world to join in and belong.

So if you feel lonely or gloomy one day,
Just peek in the flowers where fun comes to play.
For the magic they weave is not just a jest,
But a blooming mirage, in which we can rest.

Wings of the Heart

With wings made of colors, they flutter with zeal,
Bringing sunshine and giggles wherever they wheel.
Like tiny comedians in intricate flight,
They tickle the blossoms, oh what a sight!

In a frenzy of laughter, they doddle and spin,
Provoking the daisies to chuckle and grin.
They dance on the breeze with such rhythm and flair,
A heartwarming jest, a whimsical affair.

Their antics are charming, they stir up delight,
Painting the world in a playful light.
With every soft flutter, they play their own part,
Creating a symphony, wings of the heart.

So let's join the frolic, the fun, and the cheer,
Where colors and laughter are all that we hear.
For in this grand garden, so lively and bright,
Are those who spread joy with their whimsical flight.

The Harmony of Nature's Dancers

In the garden where chaos swings,
Little dancers in bright costumes flings.
They twirl and sway, oh what a scene,
Wings sparkling like a disco queen.

The prancing petals giggle with glee,
While the earthworms roll, just as happy as can be.
A ladybug drops in for the show,
With a somersault, stealing the glow!

Bumblebees buzz with a rhythm so sweet,
Dancing on daisies, oh, what a treat!
They trip on their dance, a clumsy affair,
But who can complain when there's fun in the air?

Nature watches, chuckling in delight,
As the garden throws its own bubbly night.
With laughter and twirls, what a grand spread,
In the land where the clumsy and cute dread!

Whispers of Delicate Wings

In the breeze, whispers flit and glide,
With colors so bright, they take us for a ride.
One trips over petals, the crowd all gasps,
As laughter erupts from the flowers' clasp.

A painter's palette lost in the night,
They tickle the blooms, what a comical sight!
With their fashion of hiccups and sudden turns,
Nature's own jesters wear the silliest burns.

They giggle at bees, those busy little mates,
Who stumble on nectar while sealing their fates.
The petals all cheer, flapping in applause,
For the show they present, without any pause.

Underneath the sun, it's a carnival spree,
With critters and plants dancing with glee.
When delicate wings collide with surprise,
Nature laughs loudly, no need for disguise!

Garden of Velvet Dreams

In a garden dense with feathery flair,
The blooms are debating who's most debonair.
One claims the crown for the brightest and best,
While the moon overhears, wishing for rest.

A furry old bug with a monocle perched,
Judges the scene while the petals are lurching.
As glasses clink softly, the air fills with cheer,
While a sunflower giggles, shedding a tear.

"Who spritzed my blooms with this silly perfume?"
Complains a shy bloom, feeling the gloom.
But then all at once comes a fluttering zeal,
As friend after friend take the stage for a reel.

Nature's own riot, an elegant mess,
With laughter and dances, they surely impress.
In this velvet realm, where dreams take their flight,
Every wink and a twinkle feels utterly right!

Petals in Flight

Oh, what a day for a petal parade,
As bright colors leap, they are unafraid.
Twisting and turning, a floral charade,
They giggle and tumble, quite undismayed.

With a flick and a flutter, they zip through the air,
Dodging a raindrop without any care.
A flowerhead tumbles, suffering a plight,
But finds it quite funny, and laughs at the height!

While ants join the fun with a synchronized march,
Encouraged by blooms, they leap and then arch.
A dance-off erupts while the sun takes its throne,
As petals dive and prance, never alone.

When twilight comes round, they gather in glee,
Grateful for laughter, a petal jubilee.
The night air is filled with a soft, merry sound,
As petals in flight find joy all around!

Wings of a Painted Moment

In gardens bright, they dance and spin,
Colors clash, where do I begin?
With flaps and flutters, they tickle my nose,
Who knew the world had such fancy prose?

A twist, a turn, a gentle tease,
They sip on nectar with such great ease.
Wings tickle laughter in the sun's warm blaze,
"Careful," I shout, "this isn't a maze!"

They waltz with petals, a cheeky affair,
I'm caught in a giggle, can't help but stare.
"No swatting!" I yell, "You're here for a jest!"
In this mad floral dance, I feel truly blessed.

With whispers of color, they flirt in the air,
An orchestra of giggles, it's beyond compare.
Their painted antics, a dazzling display,
In this garden, I'm the one who's gone astray!

A Symphony of Florals

Under the sun, blooms sit in rows,
A clumsy dance, just look at them pose!
Their petals sway to a silent tune,
We laugh as they sway, like a wild cartoon.

In a pot nearby, a peacock prances,
While a ladybug leads a waltz with glances.
"Please don't squish me, I'm just a guest!"
A flower shouts out, looking quite stressed!

Butterflies giggle, they do what they want,
With an air of a diva, it's hard not to flaunt.
"Is this a gay ball?" I ask with a grin,
"Or just flower power letting the fun begin?"

They flutter and tumble, a colorful scheme,
In this floral circus, I'm caught in a dream.
It's a riot of laughter, a pure delight,
In a symphony of petals, joy takes flight!

The Art of Fragile Journeys

Along the garden's whimsical lane,
They navigate with elegance, not a hint of pain.
A mission for sweetness, they flap and twirl,
In a world of clumsy, where chaos can swirl.

With each tiny dip, they make quite a scene,
Like aerobatic stars, both funny and keen.
"Watch out!" I declare, as they buzz by fast,
Creating a ruckus, oh, how long will it last?

Their antics are bold, with no hint of fear,
"Oh dearies, be careful!" I shout from here!
They dive into blooms, a thrilling parade,
In this garden of giggles, the fun never fades.

One crumples the petals, a comedic blunder,
As flowers giggle, I can't help but wonder.
In fragile journeys, they fly with such glee,
It's art for the heart, delightful and free!

Vivid Encounters

Curious colors dip and dive,
Into the bloom where dreams come alive.
"Are you lost?" I ask with a chuckle of glee,
As they flitter and flutter, just wild and free.

With a wink and a nudge, they land for a snack,
Then zip away laughing, not looking back.
"Be careful!" I shout, "There's trouble ahead!"
In a world full of petals, who needs a bed?

Colors collide like laughter in flight,
Kaleidoscope laughter, a truly wild sight.
As they dance through the blooms, all sunny and bright,
My heart takes a leap under the warm light.

The antics of colors are a joy to unfold,
With whimsy as vibrant as secrets retold.
In vivid encounters, we weave such delight,
In gardens of laughter, we twirl till the night!

A Blossom's Whisper

In the garden where beauty plays,
A flower tickles the sun's warm rays.
Petals giggle, a colorful tease,
Dancing in the wind with utmost ease.

A buzzing rhyme from a nearby bee,
Poking fun at the shy old tree.
"Hey there, trunk! You're looking quite stiff!"
"Join the party! Don't be a miff!"

Colors clash in a vivid parade,
Each plant boasting of the best charade.
They laugh and prance, it's a playful sight,
A comedy show, morning to night.

When petals fall, like playful jokes,
Sprinkling laughter among the folks.
In this patch of charm, all are elite,
Where nature's humor can't be beat.

Fluttering Thoughts

Wings of whimsy in the bright blue air,
A frolic of colors beyond compare.
Each flap a giggle, each twist a grin,
They swirl and twirl, letting joy begin.

A ticklish breeze, a cheeky wind,
Whispers of mischief where giggles blend.
"Catch me if you can!" they tease with flair,
As they flit through flowers without a care.

Sunshine winks in a lively jest,
Encouraging antics, a playful fest.
The dance of whimsy on a bright stage,
Turning each petal into a page.

With every flutter, laughter spirals,
In this garden of giggles and smiles.
Life's a riot among the blooms,
With every breath, joy simply looms.

Hues of Enchantment

A snicker of color in the grand display,
Each hue has a joke in its own way.
Pea-green whispers and rosy banter,
A punchline self-spoken in every canter.

Violet chuckles with a berry bright,
"Watch me strut, I'm the star tonight!"
While yellow bobs, doing the twist,
Saying, "Catch my rays, you can't resist!"

In their own world, they go about,
Joking of gardens, and never a doubt.
A canvas of laughter from the ground up,
Sipping on sunshine from a sipping cup.

With petals in giggles, they sway and spin,
Making the fun in each little grin.
Colors collide in riotous cheer,
Painting the path of joy far and near.

Blooming Whispers

In a patch where blossoms share a tale,
Jokes bloom softly like a morning gale.
Each bud is a bard in a floral show,
Spreading smiles wherever they grow.

Tall stems whisper secret puns,
Joining the laughter, everyone runs.
"Watch your step! I'm a slippery dew!"
Each droplet giggles, with tales anew.

Breezes play tag with the petals so light,
Racing through colors, a whimsical sight.
"Let's spin and twirl in this sunshine glow!"
As laughter echoes, they put on a show.

From seedling to bloom, they flourish with glee,
Spreading their joy, wild and free.
In this floral fantasy, joy's the key,
Where every green leaf has a joke, you see!

Essence of the Late Summer

In the garden where we roam,
Bees and blooms make quite a home.
A bug in shades of orange glows,
Dancing on a nose, who knows?

Petals whisper, 'Come and play!'
With laughter bright, we'll waste the day.
A tour of colors, sweet and bold,
And giggles where the stories unfold.

Wiggly worms with silly hats,
Critique the blooms as chitchat chats.
They wiggle and they squirm around,
In this lush kingdom, joy is found.

The sun dips low as shadows tease,
Leaves rustle softly in the breeze.
In this splendid, giggly sight,
Nature's fun is pure delight!

Floral Tides

A sea of petals, soft like cream,
Where breezes giggle and frequently scheme.
The daisies poke their heads up high,
Waving at clouds sailing by.

In this realm of sprightly cheer,
A sleeping snail snores—oh dear!
As butterflies sip from a candy cup,
They twirl and spin, never let up.

The rose's scent is quite a tease,
While other blooms wave in the breeze.
Who knew such fun could grow in rows?
Nature's laughter simply flows.

From morning's light to evening's glow,
The garden dances, putting on a show.
And every petal hides a grin,
In floral tides, where joy begins!

Wings Among Petals

Oh, what a sight with wings so bright,
They flit around, a comic flight.
One landed on a dapper shoe,
And posed like, 'Look at me, aren't you?'

In the midst of blooms so fair,
They play a game, 'Catch me if you dare!'
With giggles shared among the flowers,
They sprout their jokes in sunny hours.

A ladybug with a sly little wink,
Tells tales of petals over a drink.
Each color shines like laughter's cheer,
A gathering of joy that lingers near.

So behold the comedy of light,
As wings dance softly, day and night.
In this riot of blooms, funny and free,
We find our smiles, just you and me!

The Nature of Elegance

In gardens dressed in vibrant hues,
Nature throws a party, who'd refuse?
With sassy blooms and flirty leaves,
The style here never deceives.

Gentle sways and breezy spins,
Fashion's flair draws goofy grins.
A would-be queen, a daisy bold,
Claims the spotlight, a sight to behold.

Minty scents in full parade,
The grandest show, no masquerade.
Chic and silly, all in sight,
Their antics sparkle in the light.

With every bloom dressed to the nines,
Nature's runway has no confines.
In a dance of elegance so spry,
A blooming laughter makes us sigh!

Floral Serenade

In the garden, colors collide,
Petals sway with comical pride.
A bee trips over a flower's shoe,
Buzzing loudly, "What's a bee to do?"

The stems stand tall, a wobbly dance,
With nature's grace, they take a chance.
A snail slides by with a jaunty hat,
Claiming, "I'm the fastest in this spat!"

The daisies giggle, swaying with glee,
While clumsy ants just can't agree.
One slips and tumbles—oh what a sight,
"Is this the path to the flower's delight?"

In this lively patch, joy does bloom,
Among the laughter, there's no gloom.
Each petal whispers secrets to share,
In a floral world, love fills the air.

The Vibrant Veil

A flutter here, a twirl there,
Fashion statements fill the air.
Wings of color, a runway dance,
Models posing—what a chance!

With laughter bright and chubby cheeks,
The garden's got the latest leaks.
Giggling gusts tease the attire,
A rosebud whispers, "I'll take you higher!"

A ladybug in shades so bold,
Struts her stuff, breaking the mold.
"Who needs a ball? I'm here to flaunt!
Catch me if you can, I'm on a jaunt!"

The vines twist in a playful cheer,
Nature's party is drawing near!
With each flight, the fun expands,
In this vibrant realm, joy just stands.

Blossoms and Breezes

In the garden, where mischief brews,
Petals tease with playful hues.
A breeze pops by, just to say,
"Hey flowers, time to dance today!"

The tulips giggle, watching the show,
While winds assist with their fancy flow.
"Twist and shout, show those roots!"
While ants insist, "We've got the boots!"

Dancing daisies, round and bright,
"Watch our moves, we're quite the sight!"
Afternoon sun with a wink and a grin,
"More antics, please! Let the fun begin!"

With every sway, hearts take flight,
In this cheerful, sunny light.
The world's a stage, come one, come all,
For laughter and blooms, let's have a ball!

Transformation in Bloom

Once just a bud, now a grand surprise,
With swirling colors and twinkling eyes.
A tiny creature, what's that you see?
A fashionista in full jubilee!

Wings adorned like Sunday best,
"I'm here to party, I'll never rest!"
Amidst the petals where giggles flare,
"I'll dance with the sun, and tease the air!"

In silly spins, the garden thrives,
Creatures prance, oh how it jives!
With splashes of color, nature's jest,
Every bloom plays host to the fest!

So join the fun, embrace the scene,
With whimsy and laughter, forever keen.
In each soft whisper, the world rejoices,
With the playful blooms, we all have choices!

Love in a Garden Canvas

In the yard, where colors clash,
Dancing bugs make quite a splash,
Petals giggle in the breeze,
While bees play tag with silly ease.

Worms wear hats, it's quite a sight,
Chasing shadows, day turns night,
A daisy winks, a tulip sighs,
While grasshoppers wear goofy ties.

The ladybugs spin on their toes,
As laughter tickles all the rows,
With every rustle, joy expands,
Creating chaos on the strands.

So plant a dream in soil so bright,
And let your heart take happy flight,
In this patch of whimsy's grace,
Love blooms with a playful face.

Whimsical Moments

Among the blooms, a party starts,
With petals dancing, silly arts,
The daisies tell the tulips jokes,
While they giggle 'bout the folks.

A butterfly wears socks too tight,
Prancing around, what a funny sight,
It trips on dew, falls with a smirk,
And lands right where the critters lurk.

Crickets croon a silly tune,
As bees conduct under the moon,
The flowers cheer, they sing along,
To the nature's symphonic song.

In this garden, joy prevails,
Where humor weaves through leafy trails,
For in the laughter and the cheer,
The heart finds bliss, the soul feels clear.

Nature's Canvas Unfurled

On a canvas wide, colors explode,
With fluttering friends, laughter flowed,
Dandelions wear their fairy crowns,
As squirrels trot in tiny gowns.

A bumblebee winks at a rose,
"Why be prickly? Let's strike a pose!"
The daisies clap, the peonies sway,
Join in the revelry of the day.

The earthworms hold a dance-off show,
While ants march rugged, in a row,
With sauces made from morning dew,
They feast on air, oh what a view!

In this garden, joy is the rule,
With each petal, it's nature's school,
Where laughter springs from every nook,
And silliness fills every nook.

The Silent Song of the Meadow

In meadows wide, where mischief grows,
The flowers gossip, nobody knows,
A butterfly slides down the slide,
While a snail serves as a joyful guide.

Mice don tiny capes, take off in style,
Skip through blooms with carefree smiles,
A grasshopper plays a tambourine,
Laughing 'til it becomes quite keen.

Twinkle toes on leaves that sway,
Chanting sweetly in a playful way,
With tickled petals that shyly blush,
The breeze whispers secrets in a rush.

In the hush of this sunny space,
Every heart finds its funny trace,
And in the joy of nature's gleam,
We chase delight, pursue a dream.